AMAZING
STADIUMS

Ian Graham

amicus

mankato, minnesota

Published by Amicus
P.O. Box 1329, Mankato, Minnesota 56002

Printed in the United States of America at Corporate Graphics, in North Mankato, Minnesota.

Published by arrangement with the Watts Publishing Group Ltd., London.

Library of Congress Cataloging-in-Publication Data
Graham, Ian, 1953-
  Amazing stadiums / Ian Graham.
     p. cm. -- (Superstructures)
  Summary: "Describes some of the largest and most famous stadiums ever built. Includes information on the architects, the challenges they faced, and statistics of the finished stadiums"--Provided by publisher.
  Includes index.
  ISBN 978-1-60753-131-9 (library binding)
  1. Stadiums--Design and construction--Juvenile literature. I. Title.
  TH4714.G73 2011
  725'.827--dc22
                                        2009044043

Editor: Michael Downey
Art Direction: Harleen Mehta (Q2AMedia)
Designer: Tarang Saggar (Q2AMedia)
Picture Researcher: Kamal Kumar (Q2AMedia)
Illustrators: Sibi ND and Danish Zaidi (Q2AMedia)

Picture credits:
t=top b=bottom c=center l=left r=right

Cover: John Wang/ Photodisc/ Photolibrary: Front, Djapeman/ Shutterstock: Back
Title Page: www.sdp-photo.com
Losevsky Pavel/ Shutterstock: 3 bg., Herbert Spichtinger/ Zefa/ Corbis: 4, Jonathan Larsen/ Shutterstock: 5cl, Michael Effler/ Shutterstock: 5cr, www.sdp-photo.com: 6, 7br, Bettmann/ Corbis: 7t, Tony Ding/ Icon SMI/ Corbis: 8, David Bergman/ Corbis: 9, Bettmann/ Corbis: 10, Scott Boehm/ Getty Images: 11c, Aerial Archives/ Alamy: 12, Bob Thomas/ Getty Images: 13, Philip Gould/ Corbis: 14, Tami Chappell/ Reuters: 15t, Pool/ Getty Images: 15bl, Franck Seguin/ TempSport/ Corbis: 16, Bernard Annebicque/ SYGMA/ Corbis: 17, Scott Boehm/ Getty Images: 18, Pool/ Getty Images: 19cr, Franz-Marc Frei/ Corbis: 20, Stefan Matzke / Sampics/ Corbis: 21t, Alexandra Winkler/ Reuters: 21br, Charles Bowman/ Photolibrary: 22, Mike Hewitt/ Getty Images: 23, Christopher Lee/ Getty Images: 24, Grant Smith/ View Pictures/ Rex Features: 25br, Feng Liu/ 123rf: 26, Gideon Mendel/ Corbis: 27cr, View Stock/ Photolibrary: 27b, LRSDC: 28.

Q2AMedia Art Bank: 5br, 11b, 15cr, 19br, 25c, 27t, 29.

Note to parents and teachers:
Every effort has been made by the publishers to ensure that the web sites in this book are suitable for children, that they are of the highest educational value, and that they contain no inappropriate or offensive material.
However, because of the nature of the Internet, it is impossible to guarantee that the contents of these sites will not be altered. We strongly advise that Internet access is supervised by a responsible adult.

1210
32010

9 8 7 6 5 4 3 2 1

CONTENTS

EARLY STADIUMS

A **stadium** is a structure where people watch sports being played. The field where the games are played is surrounded by seats for spectators. Some stadiums are also used for music concerts. Stadiums are mainly for outdoor sports, while **arenas** are usually for indoor sports. The biggest sports stadium in the world is the May Day Stadium in Pyongyang, the capital city of North Korea. It can hold 150,000 people.

AMADZING FACTS

The oldest-known stadium was built at Olympia in ancient Greece. The **Olympic Games**, one of four ancient games held in Greece, were held there beginning in 776 B.C.

There are stories of the Colosseum stadium in Rome, Italy, being flooded with water so that battles between ships could be held there.

More than 250 stadiums were built across the Roman Empire.

The ancient Greek stadium built at Delphi 2,500 years ago had seating for 6,500 people.

Running Tracks

The first stadiums were built in ancient Greece. The word "stadium" comes from the Greek word *stadia*, which is a length of about 604 feet (184 m). This was the length of a race watched by people surrounding the running track. Where possible, these stadiums were built in natural hollows, with the running track at the bottom of the slopes. This allowed people at the back to see the races over the heads of the people in front of them.

Gladiators and Beasts

The ancient Romans built stadiums, too. The most famous is the Colosseum in Rome. Built in A.D. 80, portions still stand today. It is 620 feet (189 m) long by 512 feet (156 m) wide. Its outer wall stands 157 feet (48 m) high. Inside, an oval area is surrounded by rows of seating. Spectators were entertained by contests between gladiators. Wild animals from Africa, which spectators had not seen before, were brought in to fight each other or brave men.

The Colosseum in ancient Rome held as many as 50,000 spectators.

CONSTRUCTION MATERIALS

The first stadiums were made of grass or stone seating around a dirt running track. The Romans introduced **concrete** as a building material. The Colosseum was built from brick, stone, and concrete. Today, stadiums are built from many materials including steel, concrete, glass, and plastic. Clever use of these materials helps designers to create amazing new stadiums.

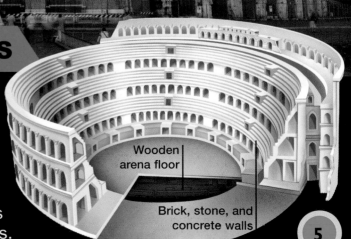

Wooden arena floor

Brick, stone, and concrete walls

MELBOURNE CRICKET GROUND

Melbourne Cricket Ground is located in Yarra Park in the Australian city of Melbourne. It is the largest sports stadium in Australia and the eighth biggest in the world. It is known to Australians as "the MCG" or just "the G." Cricket and Australian Rules Football are both played there. Music concerts are held too. It is often said to be the home of Australian sports. It hosted the 1956 Olympic Games and the 2006 Commonwealth Games. It houses Australia's National Sports Museum.

FACT FILE

- Capacity: 100,000 spectators
- Where in the world: Melbourne, Australia
- When built: 1854 (without public stand)
- Designed by: Various architects
- Playing surface: Grass

Floodlights were added to Melbourne Cricket Ground in 1985.

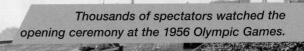

Continuous Seating

The MCG was built over more than 150 years. The first public **stand** was a wooden structure built in 1861 for 6,000 people. Eventually, all the separate stands were joined together to form continuous seating all around the field. The stadium's **capacity** of 100,000 is made up of 95,000 seats, most under cover, and 5,000 standing-room spaces.

Metal and Glass

A major redevelopment of the stadium began in 2002. More than half of it was rebuilt. Three of the old spectator stands were demolished and new stands were built in time for the Commonwealth Games in 2006. A new part-metal, part-glass roof was added, making the seating area brighter and letting in more light for the grass.

The stadium's new roof contains up to 1,213 tons (1,100 t) of steel held up by 3.3 miles (5.3 km) of cable.

MICHIGAN STADIUM

Michigan Stadium is the University of Michigan's football stadium. It is also known as the Big House to fans of its home team, the Wolverines. Michigan Stadium and Beaver Stadium in Pennsylvania have both held the title of the biggest U.S. football stadium at different times. Each has been expanded several times to hold more spectators. The latest expansion at Michigan Stadium will increase its seating capacity to more than 108,000 by 2010, making it the biggest stadium again.

The University of Michigan's football stadium is a spectacular sight from the air.

FACT FILE

- Capacity: 107,501 spectators
- Where in the world: Ann Arbor, Michigan
- When built: 1927
- Designed by: Bernard Green
- Playing surface: Artificial grass

Fans cheer on their teams in the bowl-shaped Big House stadium.

Second to None

U.S. college football grew in popularity in the early 1920s. Because of this, many colleges built stadiums with 50,000 seats or more. Far more people wanted to watch University of Michigan football games than their 42,000-seat stadium, Ferry Field, could hold. The university's football coach, Fielding Yost, suggested building a new stadium that would be second to none. The university authorities agreed and named Bernard Green as chief **architect**. The stadium he designed is still a favorite with fans.

AMAZING FACTS

The biggest crowd ever to pack into Michigan Stadium was 112,118. This was on November 22, 2003, for a football game between the Wolverines and the Ohio State team.

Scoreboards are 79 feet (24 m) wide and 39 feet (12 m) high. Each weighs more than 24 tons (22 t).

Building the Big House

Bernard Green's design for a football-only stadium combined a large seating capacity with low cost, and it was easy to build. Construction work began in 1926. The stadium opened the following year.

Michigan Stadium was constructed in a natural hollow in the ground.

Draining the Swamp

The place selected for the new stadium was swampy, so the land had to be drained. The stadium was built in a natural hollow in the ground. The bottom of the hollow was dug out to change it to the shape needed for the stadium. In the original design, the playing surface was 49 feet (15 m) below ground level, but the ground was so wet that it was raised about 6 feet (2 m). In the 1920s, when the stadium was built, this digging work was done by steam-powered shovels. Lighting was brought in so that the work could go on all day and all night.

Preparing for Growth

Coach Fielding Yost wanted Michigan's new stadium to be big enough to seat at least 100,000 people, but the university authorities decided on 72,000 seats. During construction, however, extra supports called **footings** were set in the ground for thousands more seats. This ensured that it would be easy to increase the stadium's seating capacity in later years. The first **terraces** built for the seating were made from concrete and steel laid directly on top of the sloping ground around the playing surface. The seating was made of California Redwood.

Plastic Grass

The stadium had a natural grass playing surface until 1969, when it was replaced with **artificial grass**. Natural grass was tried again beginning in 1991, but it did not grow well. In 2003, it was replaced with a new artificial surface made of plastic grass. This is more expensive to lay than natural grass, but it is harder wearing and needs less work. More and more stadiums, especially in the United States, are installing artificial grass playing surfaces.

A steel frame supports the weight of the extra seating added to Michigan Stadium in 2008.

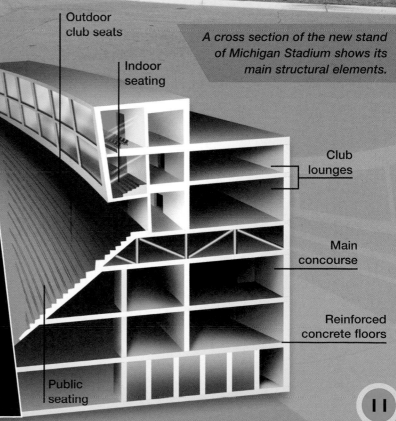

AMAZING FACTS

Underground springs turned the ground to quicksand during construction work. A steam shovel sank into the ground and is said to still be underneath the stadium today!

During the excavation work for the stadium, 200 workers removed up to 2,616 cubic yards (2,000 cu m) of earth a day.

If all the wooden seating in the original stadium was laid end to end, it would be 22 miles (35 km) long.

A cross section of the new stand of Michigan Stadium shows its main structural elements.

Outdoor club seats

Indoor seating

Club lounges

Main concourse

Reinforced concrete floors

Public seating

AZTEC STADIUM

The Aztec Stadium, or Estadio Azteca, in Mexico City is the fifth-largest stadium in the world. So far, it is the only stadium to stage two **World Cup** soccer competitions, in 1970 and 1986. It has hosted a variety of big sporting events, including the 1968 Summer Olympic Games and the 1975 Pan American Games. It is the home stadium of the Club America soccer team and the Mexican national soccer team. Because of its great size, its nickname is the Colossus of Saint Ursula. Saint Ursula is the part of Mexico City where the stadium is located.

The Aztec Stadium is supported by a ring of concrete pillars.

FACT FILE

- Capacity: 105,000 spectators
- Where in the world: Mexico City, Mexico
- When built: 1966
- Designed by: Pedro Ramirez Vazquez and Rafael Mijares Alcerra
- Playing surface: Grass

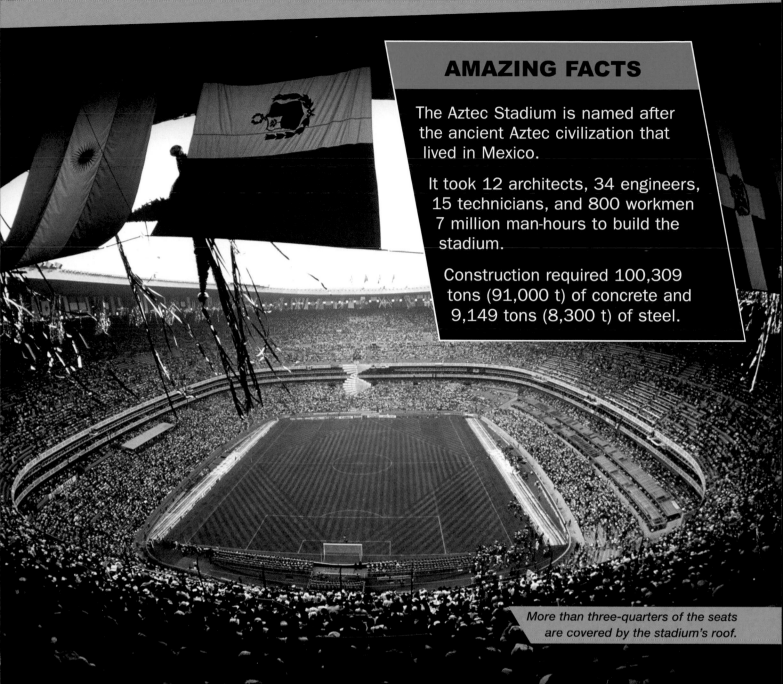

The Aztec Stadium is named after the ancient Aztec civilization that lived in Mexico.

It took 12 architects, 34 engineers, 15 technicians, and 800 workmen 7 million man-hours to build the stadium.

Construction required 100,309 tons (91,000 t) of concrete and 9,149 tons (8,300 t) of steel.

More than three-quarters of the seats are covered by the stadium's roof.

Rock Solid

Stadium builders usually have to dig down to find solid rock for a stadium's **foundation** to sit on. The Aztec Stadium's builders had no difficulty finding rock. The stadium is built on top of lava that flowed from a nearby volcano. Before construction work could begin, the rock was tested to find out how strong it was. The surface was full of cracks and holes, so 198,416 tons (180,000 t) of rock was blasted out to reach a more solid surface.

Avoiding the Sun

The playing surface is 30 feet (9 m) below street level. A good drainage system means that the field does not flood and a game can be played within minutes of a heavy downpour. The field, which is surrounded by three levels, or tiers, of seating, was positioned so that neither team is blinded as the sun crosses the sky.

LOUISIANA SUPERDOME

The Superdome is an unmistakable landmark on the New Orleans skyline.

The Louisiana Superdome is an indoor sports stadium and convention center in New Orleans, Louisiana. When it was built, it was the biggest domed structure in the world. It is still the largest steel dome. The dome is 679 feet (207 m) across and rises to a height of 272 feet (83 m). It is so famous that it is usually known simply as the Superdome or the Dome.

FACT FILE
- Capacity: 72,968 spectators
- Where in the world: New Orleans, Louisiana
- When built: 1975
- Designed by: Curtis & Davis
- Playing surface: Artificial grass

Whatever the weather, spectators inside the Superdome sit in air-conditioned comfort.

Heat and Rain

The Superdome was built to bring NFL (National Football League) football to New Orleans. The city is very hot and often experiences thunderstorms, so a weatherproof dome design was chosen. The Superdome hosts football, basketball, baseball, music concerts, and conventions. The number of seats depends on what it is used for. It has a maximum seating capacity of 72,968 for football games, 63,525 for baseball, and 85,000 for concerts.

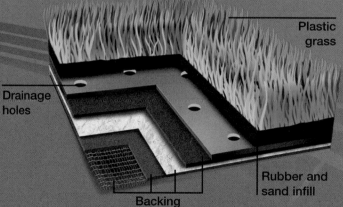

The Superdome's artificial grass is laid on a layer of sand and rubber with a tough backing to give it extra strength.

Plastic grass

Drainage holes

Rubber and sand infill

Backing

Roof Damage

The roof of the Superdome was designed to withstand winds up to 199 miles (320 km) per hour. In 2005, approximately 30,000 people were sheltered in the Superdome when Hurricane Katrina struck New Orleans and flooded the city.

The Superdome's roof was damaged by Hurricane Katrina in 2005.

STADE DE FRANCE

The *Stade de France* was built for the 1998 soccer World Cup. Its designers were given the task of creating a stadium to hold 80,000 people, all seated and all with a roof over their heads. It was the first soccer stadium built by the French government in 70 years. It can hold soccer and rugby matches, as well as music concerts.

FACT FILE

- Capacity: 80,000 spectators
- Where in the world: Paris, France
- When built: 1998
- Designed by: Michel Macary, Aymeric Zubléna, Michel Regembal, and Claude Constantini
- Playing surface: Grass

Speedy Work

The *Stade de France* was built very quickly. The excavation needed to get the site ready for construction was finished in only five months. The concrete construction took just a year. Installing the roof, seating, and technical systems took another year. The tinted-glass 14,330 ton (13,000 t) roof is designed to block the red light in sunlight, but let through blue and green light, which the grass field needs for healthy growth.

Sliding Seating

When the stadium hosts a track and field event, the lowest part of the seating is moved back to reveal a running track and landing pits underneath. It takes 80 hours to move the stand and convert the soccer stadium. The field is changed several times a year, depending on the events taking place in the stadium. It takes eight days to prepare the ground and lay a new field.

At dusk, with the lights on, the stadium's roof seems to float above the rest of the structure.

AMAZING FACTS

The stadium's design and construction needed 40,000 drawings.

During construction, 1,046,360 cubic yards (800,000 cu m) of earth was excavated.

235,431 cubic yards (180,000 cu m) of concrete and 35,275 tons (32,000 t) of steel were used in the stadium.

LOWERING THE FIELD

Some stadium designers lower the playing surface below ground level. The *Stade de France's* field is 36 feet (11 m) below ground. The easiest way to construct a stadium would be to build it on top of the ground. However, this would make some stadiums too high. They might not fit in with surrounding buildings, or they may spoil the view across the city. This is why a stadium is sometimes lowered several feet into the ground.

RELIANT STADIUM

The Reliant Stadium is the home of the Houston, Texas, football team. But it is also used for a variety of other events, including rodeos, basketball, wrestling, concerts, and conferences. It stands in Reliant Park in Houston, Texas, alongside the Reliant Arena and Astrodome. It is the biggest indoor air-conditioned space in Texas and the biggest meeting place in the state. Its most notable feature is its sliding roof.

FACT FILE
- Capacity: 71,500 spectators
- Where in the world: Houston, Texas
- When built: 2002
- Designed by: HSC and HOK Sport
- Playing surface: Grass

The stadium has been cleverly designed. Every spectator has an uninterrupted view of the field.

Hot and Cold

Houston's Reliant Stadium is the first stadium in the National Football League to have a **retractable roof**. As the stadium would be used for events in winter, it was decided to build a roof that could be opened in good weather and closed in bad weather. A powerful air-conditioning system keeps the stadium comfortably cool on hot days.

Moving the Roof

The vast roof covering is made of **fiberglass**, which is a very lightweight material. The roof opens in the middle and the two halves slide apart. They move on electrically driven wheels that run along tracks. The roof panels are locked safely in position when they are not moving.

The stadium's fiberglass roof was damaged by Hurricane Ike in 2008.

RETRACTABLE ROOFS

Stadiums covered with domes were popular in the 1960s and 1970s. They let audiences watch outdoor sports in comfort regardless of the weather. However, a dome cuts out too much light for grass to grow well. Stadiums with retractable roofs solve this problem. A retractable roof can be left open to let grass inside the stadium grow well, but closed when there is bad weather during an event.

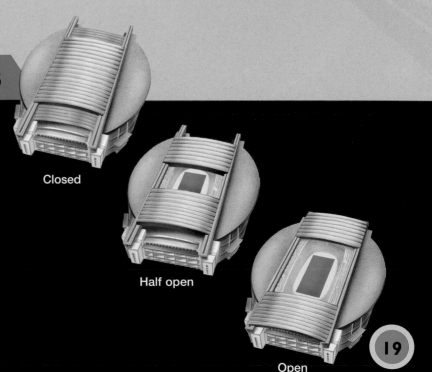

Closed

Half open

Open

ALLIANZ ARENA

The Allianz Arena is the first stadium in the world that can change color at the press of a button. The color of the stadium is changed depending on which home soccer team is playing. It is red when Bayern Munich is playing, blue when TSV 1860 Munich is at home, and white when the German National soccer team is on the field. Local people have nicknamed it the *Schlauchboot*, meaning inflatable boat or rubber dinghy because of its appearance.

Giant Spaceship

The stadium's steel and concrete structure is covered with 2,874 thin, see-through plastic pockets called cushions. These are permanently inflated with air. The cushions provide insulation and resist winds. They also make the stadium look like a huge spacecraft that has just touched down on the ground.

FACT FILE
- Capacity: 69,900 spectators
- Where in the world: Munich, Germany
- When built: 2005
- Designed by: Herzog and de Meuron
- Playing surface: Grass

Every spectator is covered by the self-cleaning roof.

Visual Impact

The plastic cushions that form the stadium's walls and roof are illuminated by lighting tubes. The light shines through red, blue, or clear filters. Switching to a different filter changes the color of the light shining on the cushions. When the color is changed, it is done slowly over two minutes so as not to startle or distract drivers on a nearby motorway.

During construction, the arena's roof cushions were carefully attached to the steel frame.

WEMBLEY STADIUM

Wembley Stadium is the largest soccer stadium that has every seat under cover. It stands on the site of the old Wembley Stadium, which was built in 1924. It is the most important sports and entertainment stadium in Britain. In 2003, the old stadium was demolished and the new stadium was built in its place. The new stadium is four times the height and twice the area of the old Wembley Stadium.

FACT FILE

- Capacity: 90,000 seated spectators
- Where in the world: London, England
- When built: 2007
- Designed by: Foster and Partners and HOK Sport
- Playing surface: Grass

Soaring Arch

Wembley Stadium's roof hangs from an **arch** that soars 436 feet (133m) above the stadium. The arch was carefully placed so that it never casts a shadow on the field. Using the arch to hold up part of the roof's weight means that there are no pillars inside the stadium to spoil the spectators' view. The roof is partly retractable. It is opened between events to let in light for the grass, but it can be moved so that every seated spectator is under cover.

Multipurpose Venue

Wembley Stadium was built to be Britain's most important soccer stadium. It can also hold rugby matches, football games, track and field competitions, and music concerts. For track and field events, a platform with a running track on top is built over the soccer field. The stadium's capacity ranges from 68,000 for track and field events to 105,000 for music concerts. At full capacity, 90,000 spectators can be seated and there is standing room for 15,000 people.

AMAZING FACTS

Wembley Stadium encloses a space of 5.2 million cubic yards (4 million cu m).

Each of the stadium's two giant television screens is as big as 600 home TV screens.

If all the rows of seats were placed end to end, they would form a line almost 34 miles (54 km) long.

There are 2,618 toilets in Wembley Stadium, more than any other stadium.

The roof is suspended from steel cables attached to the arch.

Monster Machine

The old Wembley Stadium had to be demolished and cleared away before work could begin on the new stadium. A huge excavator vehicle, the biggest of its type in the world, was specially built for the job. It cut the old stadium to pieces with giant crushing jaws.

Underground Supports

As the design of the stadium called for the field to be about 13 feet (4 m) below the old field, thousands of tons of soil was removed to lower the ground level. As many as 4,000 underground columns, called **piles**, were put in place. The deepest piles were driven 115 feet (35 m) into the ground. The stadium's steel frame was then built on top.

The new Wembley Stadium began to take shape amid a forest of tall cranes.

AMAZING FACTS

The stadium was built with about 25,355 tons (23,000 t) of steel.

The steel roof weighs 7,715 tons (7,000 t). The arch holds up 70 percent of this weight.

The arch weighs 1,930 tons (1,750 t), about the same as 10 jumbo jet airliners.

At 1,035 feet (315 m), the roof arch span is the longest single span roof structure in the world.

Straws and Modules

As the piles were being driven into the ground, the stadium's roof arch was being built. This was made from 500 steel tubes called straws, which are far bigger than drinking straws! The straws were connected together to make sections, called modules, 67.3 feet (20.5 m) long. The modules were linked together to form the arch. When the arch was assembled over the stadium, it could be seen from more than 12 miles (20 km) away on a clear day. The top of the arch has a bright **beacon** to make it easier for aircraft to see it at night.

Arch

Lifting cables

Restraint cables

The arch was built on the ground and then raised into position.

The piles were sunk into holes in the ground drilled by giant screw-shaped augers.

FOUNDATION

A building's foundation is the structure under the ground that supports the building's weight. A big, heavy building, such as a sports stadium, needs a deep foundation. Long legs, called piles, are sunk into the ground. The tops of the piles are then linked together with steel bars and concrete, and the stadium is built on top to make a strong and stable building.

BEIJING NATIONAL STADIUM

FACT FILE

- Capacity: 80,000 spectators
- Where in the world: Beijing, China
- When built: 2008
- Designed by: Herzog and de Meuron
- Playing surface: Grass

When China's capital city, Beijing, won the right to stage the 2008 Olympic Games, the government held a competition to find the best design for a new national stadium. Architects Herzog and de Meuron won with a stunning design that quickly became known as the **Bird's Nest**.

Inside-out Design

The stadium was designed from the inside out. The seating area for the spectators was designed first. The design ensures that spectators can be as close to the action as possible. The rest of the stadium was designed to wrap around the seating. The Bird's Nest is made of 7,500 steel "twigs." Each had to be designed separately to make sure that it curved and twisted in exactly the right way to fit perfectly. The structure stands on 24 steel supports, each weighing 1,100 tons (1,000 t).

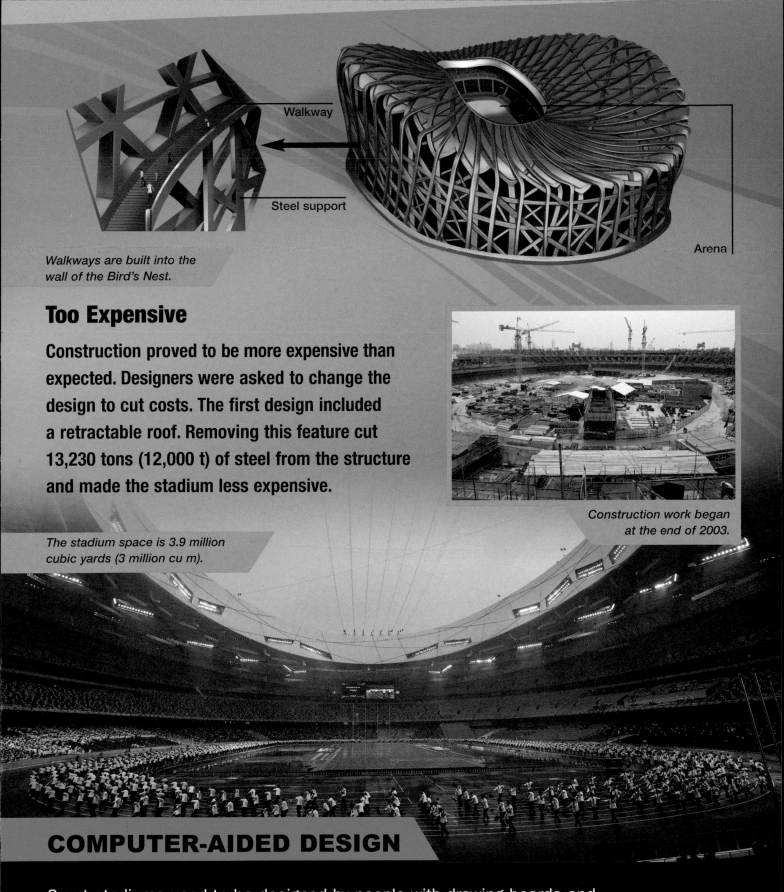

Walkway

Steel support

Arena

Walkways are built into the
wall of the Bird's Nest.

Too Expensive

Construction proved to be more expensive than
expected. Designers were asked to change the
design to cut costs. The first design included
a retractable roof. Removing this feature cut
13,230 tons (12,000 t) of steel from the structure
and made the stadium less expensive.

Construction work began
at the end of 2003.

The stadium space is 3.9 million
cubic yards (3 million cu m).

COMPUTER-AIDED DESIGN

Sport stadiums used to be designed by people with drawing boards and
slide rules. Today, they are designed using computer-aided design (**CAD**),
simulation and **visualization systems**. These can produce a lifelike picture of
the finished stadium. They can show the stadium from any angle and even
let designers fly through it like a video game. They can also test the
strength of the building and spot weaknesses before construction begins.

STADIUMS IN THE FUTURE

All over the world, dozens of new sports stadiums are now being built or are planned for the future. The design of a sports stadium is important for its success. If the design is wrong, sports fans will stay away. The location is important, too. Stadiums have to be built in the right place.

Moving into Cities

Future stadiums are not likely to be any larger than those of today. Bigger stadiums would give the spectators farthest from the action a poor view. In the past, stadiums were often built outside cities. Now, it is more common to build them in cities and make them important symbols of the city and the nation. The stadiums of the future will be stunning examples of architecture, design, and engineering. They will also reflect the history and culture of the country or area in which they are built.

An artist's impression of the new Aviva stadium in Dublin, Ireland, named after the insurance company who is sponsoring it.

Bowls of Sound

The old way to design a sports stadium was to place a field in the middle and surround it with stands for spectators. Future stadiums will not be designed in this way. Instead, they will be even more bowl-shaped than the most modern stadiums today. The shape of the walls and roof will be designed to reflect crowd noise back into the bowl to create a more exciting experience.

LONDON 2012 OLYMPIC STADIUM

Cable-supported roof

Decorated fabric curtain

55,000-seat upper tier

Upper tier framework

25,000 permanent seats

These computer-generated images of the London 2012 Olympic Stadium show the complete stadium and an exploded view of the building. After the Olympic Games, the upper tier of 55,000 seats will be removed to produce a smaller 25,000-seat stadium for the local community.

29

GLOSSARY

arch
a curved structure spanning a gap or opening that is very good for supporting the weight of a building

architect
person who designs buildings, including sports stadiums

arena
building or structure where people watch events, especially indoor sports

artificial grass
plastic playing surface made to look like natural grass

beacon
bright light or flashing light placed on top of a tall structure as a warning to pilots of nearby aircraft

Bird's Nest
nickname given to the Beijing National Stadium where the 2008 Summer Olympic Games were held

CAD
computer-aided design, a method for creating designs with computers and design software

capacity
maximum number of spectators a stadium is designed to hold

concrete
building material made from a mixture of sand, cement, gravel, and water

ETFE
ethylene tetrafluoroethylene, a strong plastic used in the construction of some sports stadiums; unlike many other plastics, ETFE is not damaged by sunlight, does not burn, and is self-cleaning

excavation
changing the level of the ground by moving earth

footings
shallow foundations

fiberglass
strong lightweight material made from hair-like strands of glass embedded in plastic

foundations
underground part of a building that supports the weight of the building

louver
thin bars or panels that can be tilted to reflect light and make a stadium appear to change color

man-hour
the amount of work one man can do in one hour

Olympic Games
international sports event held in a different country every four years

piles
underground legs or pins that form the deep foundations for a building such as a sports stadium

pillar
vertical support that holds up part of a building

retractable roof
roof that can be opened and closed

span
distance between two supports

stadium
building or structure where people gather to watch events, especially outdoor sports

stand
seating area at a stadium

terraces
usually concrete steps, with higher steps at the back where spectators can stand

tier
layer or level with each tier higher and further back than the one below it

visualization system
computer system that can create a realistic image of a new building

watt
measurement of power, a household light bulb might be 100 watts, lighting power used in some stadiums is measured in millions of watts

World Cup
international soccer competition held in a different country every four years

INDEX

WEB LINKS

www.bbc.co.uk/history/ancient/romans/colosseum_01.shtml
Everything you ever wanted to know about the Colosseum in Rome.

www.worldstadiums.com
Information about 10,000 stadiums in more than 223 countries.

http://www.london2012.com/venues/olympic-stadium.php
See what the stadium for the 2012 London Olympic Games will look like.

http://entertainment.howstuffworks.com/question591.htm
Find out how moving roofs on sports stadiums work.

http://en.beijing2008.cn/cptvenues/venues/nst/n214078095.shtml
The official web site of the 2008 Olympic games, includes many pictures of the
Beijing National Stadium.

**http://www.forbes.com/2008/03/31/sports-stadiums-yankees-biz-
sports_cx_tvr_0331stadiums.html**
View a slide show of 10 new superstadiums.